D1146440

SAY CHEESE!

COMPILED BY WESLEY DALE
ILLUSTRATED BY TUTU TYUTYUNNIK

First published in the UK in 2014 by Head of Zeus Ltd.

Feist Catalog Inc, London W1F 9LD

9 7 5 3 1 2 4 6 8

A CIP catalogue record for this book is available
from the British Library.

Hardback ISBN: 9781784081058
Printed and bound in China.

Head of Zeus Ltd
Clerkenwell House
45-47 Clerkenwell Green
London EC1R 0HT

www.headofzeus.com

WESLEY DALE is a pseudonym for a
UK fiction editor who lives in London.
Her favourite cheese is Roquefort.

TUTU TYUTYUNNIK is not a pseudonym.
She is a graphic designer and lives in London.
Her favourite cheese is Quark.

WITH THANKS TO
THE EAGLE MANSION CHEESE SUMMIT
Al, Cons, Ferdie, George,
George, Kath & Lucy.

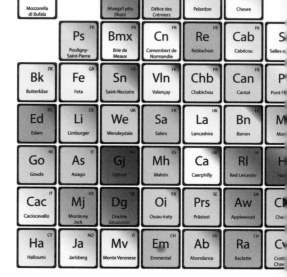

< simple

Mdb (IT) Mozzarella di Bufala	Af (ES) Afuega'l pitu (Rojo)	Dc (FR) Délice des Crémiers	Pl (FR) Pelardon	Cv (FR) Chevre		
	Ps (FR) Pouligny-Saint-Pierre	Bmx (FR) Brie de Meaux	Cn (FR) Camembert de Normandie	Re (FR) Reblochon	Cab (FR) Cabécou	S... Selles-s...
Bk (DE) Butterkäse	Fe (GR) Feta	Sn (FR) Saint-Nectaire	Vln (FR) Valençay	Chb (FR) Chabichou	Can (FR) Cantal	P... Pont-l'...
Ed (NL) Edam	Li (DE) Limburger	We (UK) Wensleydale	Sa (FR) Salers	La (UK) Lancashire	Bn (FR) Banon	M... Mo...
Go (NL) Gouda	As (IT) Asiago	Gj (FR) Gjetost	Mh (ES) Mahón	Ca (UK) Caerphilly	Rl (UK) Red Leicester	H... Ha...
Cac (IT) Caciocavallo	Mj (US) Monterey Jack	Dg (UK) Double Gloucester	Oi (FR) Ossau-Iraty	Prs (SE) Prästost	Aw (US) Applewood	C... Che...
Ha (CY) Halloumi	Ja (NO) Jarlsberg	Mv (IT) Monte Veronese	Em (CH) Emmental	Ab (FR) Abondance	Ra (CH) Raclette	Cv... Crott... Chav...

THE PERIODIC TABLE OF CHEESE
(100 cheeses version)

| P... Pec... |

complex >

soft >

< hard

| Cha [FR] Chaource | Bml [FR] Brie de Melun | Sb [UK] Stinking Bishop | Tc [ES] Torta del Casar |

...gres | Mu [FR] Munster | Se [PT] Serra da Estrela | Eb [FR] Époisses de Bourgogne | Bg [FR] Blue de Gex | Ba [FR] Bleu d'Auvergne | Ro [FR] Roquefort

...oozola | Cob [UK] Cornish Blue | Mn [DE] Montagnolo | Ne [DK] Neufchâtel | Es [DK] Esrom | Fa [FR] Fourme d'Ambert | Lv [FR] Livarot

...iggio | Gor [IT] Gorgonzola | Da [DK] Danablu | Bc [FR] Bleu des Causses | St [UK] Stilton | Db [UK] Dorset Blue Vinney | Val [ES] Valdeon

...erin ...rgeois [CH] | Cy [UK] Cornish Yarg | Ch [UK] Cheddar | Chm [UK] Cheddar (filtered) | Cc [IT] Caciotta | Mr [FR] Maroilles | Pp [IT] Provolone (Piccante)

...botten [SE] | Mw [IT] Murcian Wine Cheese | Ur [IT] Ubriaco di Rabosa | Sj [PT] São Jorge | To [IT] Toma | Sh [UK] Shropshire Blue | Fo [IT] Fontina

...s (36m) [LT] | Ma [ES] Manchego | Id [ES] Idiazabal | Cns [IT] Canestrato | Co [FR] Comté | Rg [IT] Ragusano | Og [UK] Ogleshield

...fort | Ga [NL] Gouda (aged) | Gr [CH] Gruyère | Mi [FR] Mimolette | Pr [IT] Parmigiano-Reggiano | Gp [IT] Grana Padano | Ff [IT] Formaggio di Fossa

< hard

WHAT CHEESE
LURES A GRIZZLY
OUT OF THE WOODS?

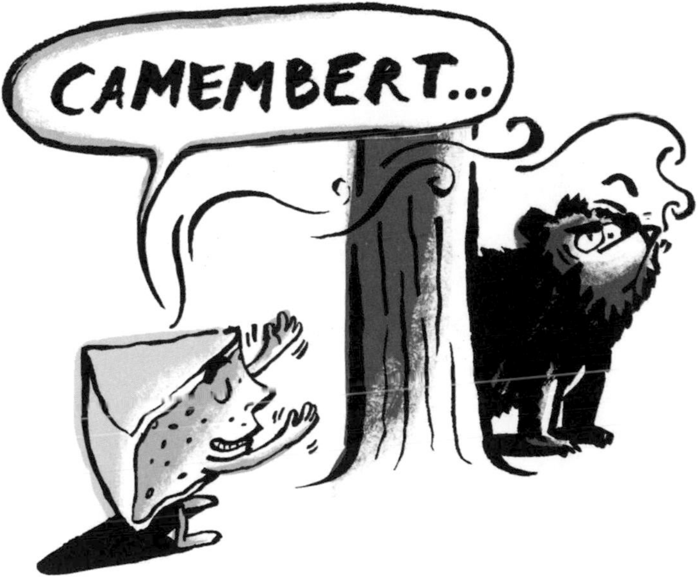
CAMEMBERT...

HOW DO THEY EAT CRUMBLY CHEESE IN WALES?

WHAT DO YOU GET IF YOU EAT TOO MUCH GREEK CHEESE?

WHAT DID THE CHEESE SAY
WHEN HE SAW HIMSELF
IN THE MIRROR?

WHAT DO YOU
CALL CHEESE THAT
ISN'T YOURS?

WHAT CHEESE
DO YOU USE TO HIDE
A SMALL HORSE?

WHAT CHEESE DO
THEY EAT IN THE
HADRON COLLIDER?

WHICH CHEESE IS MADE BACKWARDS?

WHAT'S A SPY'S FAVOURITE CHEESE?

WHAT CHEESE HIDES UNDER THE BED?

WHAT IS A CANNIBAL'S
FAVOURITE CHEESE?

WHAT CHEESE IS
INDISPENSABLE AT
THE FRENCH OPEN?

WHAT DID THE CHEESE DO WHEN THE HIPPY PLANTED IT?

WHAT CHEESE BELONGS
ON THE HANDLEBARS
OF A TINY BIKE?

WHAT DOES A CHEESE
ASK FOR WHEN HE'S
ON A PUB CRAWL?

WHAT CHEESE DO CORNISH PIRATES EAT?

WHAT CHEESE IS TARKA THE OTTER'S BEST FRIEND?

WHICH CHEESE LOVES WILD PARTIES?

WHAT CHEESE DO CYCLISTS CARRY?

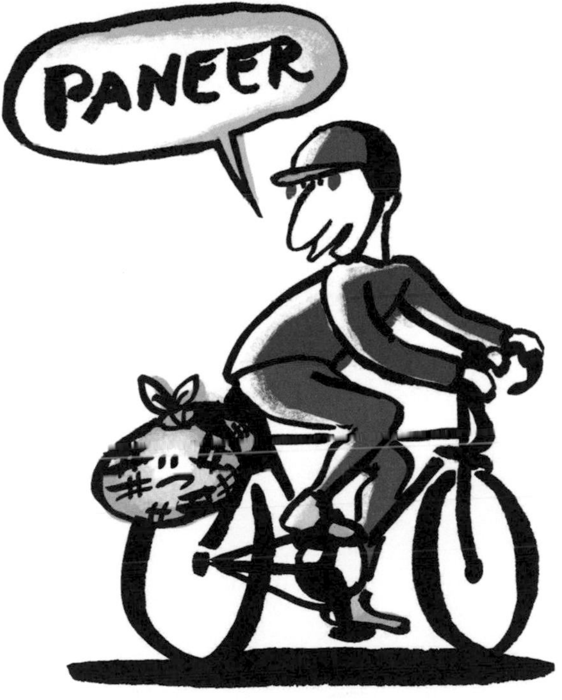
PANEER

WHAT IS DICK AND HARRY'S FAVOURITE CHEESE?

WHAT CHEESE DOES
CAMBRIDGE EAT WHEN THEY
WIN THE BOAT RACE?

WHICH CHEESE CLEARED THE CHURCH AISLES ON SUNDAY?

WHAT DO YOU GET FROM EATING TOO MUCH SWISS CHEESE?

WHAT CHEESE
IS TOO YOUNG TO
SLEEP IN THE BED?

WHAT IS SYLVESTER STALLONE'S FAVOURITE CHEESY SEQUEL?

WHICH ARE THE WINDIEST CHEESES?

WHAT DO YOU CALL AN ALCOHOLIC CHEESE?

WHAT IS A CIRCUS PERFORMER'S FAVOURITE CHEESE?

WHICH CHEESE DIDN'T LAUGH ONCE AT THE JOKES IN THIS BOOK?

Is there anything we've missed?

Email or tweet your cheese jokes to

hello@headofzeus.com
@HoZ_Books

for a chance to win...